Pass It On

Princeton Series of Contemporary Poets
For other books in the series, see page 74

Rachel Hadas

Pass It On

Princeton University Press
Princeton, New Jersey

Library of Congress Cataloging-in-Publication Data
Hadas, Rachel.
Pass it on / Rachel Hadas.
p. cm.—(Princeton series of contemporary poets)
ISBN 0-691-06761-9   ISBN 0-691-01454-X (pbk.)
I. Title. II. Series.
PS3558.A3116P37 1989
811'.54—dc19
88-31619
CIP

Publication of this book has been aided by the
Whitney Darrow Fund of Princeton University Press

This book has been composed in Linotron Galliard

Clothbound editions of Princeton University Press books
are printed on acid-free paper, and binding materials are
chosen for strength and durability.
Paperbacks, although satisfactory for personal collections,
are not usually suitable for library rebinding

Printed in the United States of America
by Princeton University Press,
Princeton, New Jersey

When will you speak again?
Our words are the children of many people.
They are sown, are born like infants,
take root, are nourished with blood.
—George Seferis, "Three Secret Poems"

For my mother, Elizabeth Chamberlayne Hadas

Contents

Acknowledgments

Many of these poems initially appeared, sometimes in slightly different form or with different titles, in the following periodicals: *Agni Review* ("The End of Summer"); *Boulevard* ("First Night Back," "Nourishment"); *Denver Quarterly* ("The Blind Gates," "Over the Edge," "Teaching the Iliad"); *Literary Review* ("Mortalities," "Odds Against," "Philoctetes"); *Margin* ("Generations"); *The New Criterion* ("Bedtime" and "Idolatry Brood," now "The Fields of Sleep," parts vi and xiii); *Partisan Review* ("Pass It On, III," "Summer in White, Green, and Black"); *PN Review* ("The Burial of Jonathan Brown"); *Sequoia* ("Fix It," parts iv and v); *Southwest Review* ("Pass It On, I"). Kind permission to reprint is acknowledged in all cases. In addition, "Hortus Conclusus" is reprinted from *PRAIRIE SCHOONER*, by permission of the University of Nebraska Press, copyright © 1989 by the University of Nebraska Press. "Three Silences" is reprinted from *Shenandoah*, The Washington and Lee University Review with the permission of the editor, copyright © 1987/1988 by Washington & Lee University. "Four Angers" was first published in *The Yale Review*, copyright © Yale University. Thanks are also due to the 1986/1987 and 1987/1988 editions of the *Anthology of Magazine Verse and Yearbook of American Poetry* (Beverly Hills, Calif.: Monitor Book Co.), where "Summer in White, Green, and Black" and "The End of Summer" appeared, and to *The Best American Poetry, 1988*, John Ashbery, editor; David Lehman, series editor (New York: Charles Scribner's Sons/Collier Books, 1988), where "Nourishment" appeared. Thanks also to Princeton University Press for their gracious permission to reprint a portion of George Seferis's "Three Secret Poems" in the Dedication.

Pass It On

I

The Fields of Sleep (Summer)

i
On a bare beach a woman and a man
ask an enormous question finally
answered and embodied in the blond
shape of a baby who is now refusing
to take an apple from her outstretched hand.

Still life: peeled pear; cheese; apple; napkin tied
bandit fashion round a little neck?
In life it's never still. You must
choose between color and order,
blood in the cheeks, the kerchief's red-white check.

Or else in white and blue
he and she sit still at the edge of a river.
Her head against his shoulder,
they picture striped umbrellas, awnings fluttering
in some country where there's still a sky.

ii
You splash in a shallow
navel of idle
pulses whose tug,
deceptively gentle,

laps at the central
cherished hollow
print of an absence,
mold you were pressed in,

and sculpts those features—
familiar, forgotten—
you recognize under
the striped umbrella,

propping the baby
against the wall
black in the sun
of the salty hole,

gulf of years
nibbled, eroded
by an invisible
undertow.

iii
What light we saw, kindled, reflected—quenched.
Our mirrors' mutual sparkling put to bed,
dully we face each other,
too tired to use the silence.
I have lost you
no more than myself.

What dove to the bottom will
resurface in brief calm,
a silver tail
gleam in sullen air.

iv
Last night we watched
a twinkling star
or flying saucer
or beacon of war

flash red, then blue,
or red, then green—
invisible through
a binocular

or under cupped hand.
Then went to bed.
Mysterious beacon.
Mysterious man,

so near and far.
Bank of warm bone.
Socked-in aircraft
or nameless star.

v

The proffered bowl of milk. A child's grave face,
attentive, listening.
A woman glimpsed through trees. How silently
she parts the branches, saving words as too
precious for any ordinary use
before the black gates close.

vi

How can I put you down?

Nightly you must negotiate alone
fluorescent escalators, straddle
banisters gleaming neon
and noiselessly slide down.

How can I tell you "sleep"?

Nightly the body yearns to re-create
its lost polarity,
shape of love unsculpted,
lost or forgotten mate.

How can I let you cry?

Nightly you must move on
toward that point where all roads come
together into one
lost just as it touches the horizon.

How can I shut the door?

Nightly you must go through
so many dark arcades
and come back whole
clutching morning's clue.

vii

Clasping her burbling radio
the old woman sleeps.
Is she a widow after twenty years?
Does anyone now love her?

The youngest one, half boy half baby, sleeps.
The man and woman
sleep back to back. Sheet lightning
flaps against the sky's dark argument.

Black scooped from silence, too
flat for reflections, summer
runs along under the bridge of night.
Mornings they rise to their names.

Having travelled the enormous distance,
they need to re-create it
not once but daily. Not
daily but nightly to go down alone.

viii

Night is stumbling over fields of thunder.
Fulgurations
soldered together might illuminate
summer as one
sunken continent of broken sleep—
now scattered islands
dipping from fitful fire.

ix

Sunday morning. Smell of something dead
rises through boards of the porch
floor where mother and son
sit dragging loaded brushes over newsprint.
Patches of red and orange wait for meaning
to dry. What lies below
rots at a sultry pace;
what lives takes shape and nods,
sleepy with summer, stubbornly still growing.

Her finger pricked, the Sleeping Beauty fell
asleep for a hundred summers
as a result of which (the child
dabbing the spindle red
adds) she felt much better.

x

Where system met
system, the old ones spoke
wordlessly, code
embedded as in rock.

Ceremony half
true, the old game
annually renewed:
song without name,

rippleable small pool,
infinitely deep
swallower of all
outrageous rigmarole

studies moth and stone,
water, flower, wood
fragrant after rain.
New, the late world.

xi
Maps and weather draw that slate-blue gaze
tracing and poring labyrinthine ways
of high cloud structures, silent omens of
remote mutations at an earthly pace.

That minatory tower of steely gray,
fog that a sullen sunrise burns away,
a rainbowed stormlet spattering at noon—
all taken from the palette of one day.

Cloud-maps combine fortuity with fate.
Lines plotted out, we scan them, stand, and wait.
Tock goes the metronome. A yawn. A sneeze.
Sun bursts through and it thunders, soon or late.

You've worked out devious ways to reach this house
cocooned in its deceptive August drowse.
The sky is azure, navy, apple green.
Infinite suspension carries us.

xii
Glory and dullness crowd the eye and ear
down to a stream of names,
desires, the bite-sized hills
closing in prematurely
like a stage setting (who turned down the lights?).

Joy and numbness split the repetition
in two; an apple
squarely slaps the pole
and shatters and the bits
roll into deep wet grass, bare hills of dream.

xiii
To gaze at the hypnotic
yellow moon of summer,
to focus on a stone,
on lives that wax and wane,
on leaves that come undone
in drought or shine with rain,
the child's fresh face, a magnet to the eye—
is this idolatry?

Between the glistening pelts of bathing children
and the knuckle-gnawing refusal
to look up from one's book,
find out some middle way.
Fences. A weathered barn.
Are you getting warmer?
The milky gray expanse of sky implodes
on one more apparition:

no silo shimmering through celestial mist,
only more love for this
world's pillars, banisters,
exit signs, arches, thresholds, winding stairs
struggled up toward a revelation hidden
even as we breathe the thinner
air and feel the sun's
last heat on our closed faces.

i

To love a son
and the moon out of darkness.
No way but words, the blind
clutch in trust, the plane
tilts over gleaming fields,
shrugs higher, and another planet rises—
no, the moon
over the mountain's shoulder, going home,
ripe orange, soon to set
above the world my own, my delicate
network of joy and fear, the week's arc done.

ii

Day by day another summer gone.
Calmly the lamp shines in a veil of rain.
Music booming in the dusty barn
as through a hole in the wall the claim
of morning keeps on shining. Leaves
turn. It doesn't rain. I turn to see
him lie a little while on the wolfskin
resting from play as sun
sneaks in the window. Boards
are gray with weather. Spiderwebs, dead flies
and wasps, and through the window
that withering and brilliance of leaves
whose workaday theatrics deck a world
yellow and black and pale and hectic red
where things go gray and spectre-thin and die.

iii

Sunsets over Lake Champlain, a mini
Mare Nostrum. Though they call the event
of a water landing (surely an oxymoron)
"extremely unlikely," nevertheless it's water
this dying light luxuriantly slides over

as the plane tilts. Two
seats ahead a pair of lovers kiss
then pull apart to gaze at one another
turning their heads unnaturally far
so each can wholly scan the other's face,
devour it all, eyes, hair, bone, breath,
penetrate the frustrate, the opaque
envelope of flesh
which will become, to one in the back seat,
a ghostly comfort—alone, not alone,
holding a hand, touching a knee, but reaching
the world at a deliberate remove
from that fresh famished love,
sensing otherness
over a bridge of bone.

iv

My little Ithaca. A gilded world,
tiny. The simple opening to receive
and closing, undramatic,
dimple in dough, ripple on brown water,
now seen, now not,
most valued at a distance.

Zone of suspension here.
Gold hole between the worlds.
Through a gap in the wall
a window in the barn
the long dull morning gliding on and on.

v

To fix the wind
or the late clouds' slate
or your sweet weight
nights on my knees;

hillside of trees
eternally plural;
autumns and suns;
memories; moons;

this orange leaf,
this brown, another.
Fullness, remember.
Fix each grief

over and over
in the heart's eye,
the eye's deep core,
scarlet of autumn

when blood and green
yearly sluice out.
I cannot do it—
cannot keep color

from sliding out
between my fingers
and clench a fist
on emptiness.

Step out to pee
in crisp grass
and there is the sound
of winter, wind

starting to sough
through almost bare
branches, stripping
naked for winter.

Fix It (Winter)

He disappeared in the dead of winter.
—W. H. Auden

lips part
To greet the perfect stranger.
—James Merrill

i

Heart's February: fill it in as bleak
and lonely. But today a warming flood
of color stains the calendar's pale cheek.
The eve of your return I give my blood.
Picture a glacier bruising into bloom.
I let it all hang out and drain from my
right, my writing arm: the silent room,
morning and evening's empty bed. I lie
between two bodies, palping a red ball,
flushed to pallor, gazing at the ceiling,
as hollow days are dammed into a crimson pool
soon to be sealed and channeled to a stranger
and even more precarious life. I'm filling
a loving cup to raise to mortal danger.

ii

What the eye, seeking, fails to penetrate
the ear awaits. Presently a cry

(baby waking, tomcat, beaten dog,
or floating rage caught raw between the walls)

shrills from the street. No, from the locked
interior whose study window, bright

with strained attention, now winks suddenly
from a blank surface. You've turned on the light.

Beyond the potted palms in some remote
anteroom the beaded curtains stir:

so I must sense, must pluck from winter air
the snatches of that song, or let the link

between our skulls (now stretched; now tighter) loosen.
I shut my eyes and almost hear you think.

iii
I read much of the night. Ineptly woo
some shabby cousin of oblivion
out of the garish hours after two.
Having locked the secret inmost door,
stretched, and remembered once again you're gone,
I wander to the kitchen for a swig
of milk, and creak back down the corridor
to a ghost bedroom, chilly and too big.

No, but the necklace! Burst
and scattered agates sprayed apart and rolled
under the furniture, and it was lost,
the labyrinth of winter, overnight
and not to be recovered. Somehow sealed
in those cold globes was a whole summer's wealth of light.

iv
I lean my ladder on
the beautiful, the flawed
handiwork of God
and turn to spy my son

busy way down there
patching a balloon,
filling in the moon.
The whole world needs repair.

Broken! he calls the moon
if it is less than round.
These syllables resound
domestically soon

as lightbulb, pencil, tile
get broken. His decree
Fix it! shows faith in me
that prompts me first to smile

and then suppress a sigh
and fetching tape and glue
climb up to mend the blue
disasters in the sky.

I lean my ladder on
the beautiful, the flawed
handiwork of God
and turn to spy my son.

v

Time to tunnel deeper into winter.
Broken! the boy cries, pointing at the moon.
Agates roll downhill into the river.

I stretch my chilly legs awake and wonder
whether this absence will seem warmer soon
and, sighing, rise: another day of winter.

It's not as if I'm lonely. I'm a mother.
busy with fixing - *pop* went that balloon.
Agates roll away into a river

opaque with ice. So walk across the water,
so fix the brownouts of a cloudy sun?
No use. We're heading deeper into winter.

What has been lost is gone and gone forever:
such knowledge is what forty winters mean.
My agates (yours?)—they vanished in the river

like last year's snows. The only ever after
is what's already written in the rune
of losses deeply etched into the winter
while agates settle blackly at the bottom of the river.

17

vi
Something terrible is going to happen.
Something terrible has already happened.

Up from the dark words of authority rise,
anger, affection. Lights

gleam a minute till the door is slammed.
Easier to instruct anyone else in the truth of feeling

than try to span the awful gap yourself,
yourself to search for stones to leapfrog on

across the—is it water or a tunnel?
And in. And shut that door.

I don't hear or listen well these days.
Did you say your new poem about your father

was to be called "Lines Found in a Bottle"?
I think I got it wrong. This bottle had

milk in it, bourbon, apple juice—not words.
It plugged three generations' mouths to dumbness.

Weaned to a cup, my son escaped the bottle
and now eats sugar by the spoonful. I chew gum.

Faces stuffed, we slam right out of this
impossible world, propelled at speed

by terror, rage, loss,
and enter the shadow room of mourning.

Now it is multiplied as in a hall of mirrors.
Unpeeled of memory, ranks of men leap up

leaving lighted rooms with a start to go
in search of those lost lives:

precious particulars of how and when,
not whether, something terrible has happened.

"Both my fathers have cancer," you said once.
I think you said it. Asymmetrically

you had two fathers, I had none. I had to
run upstairs one summer, slam a door,

and cry about my father: not that the loss was fresh
but that downstairs a woman also wept

whose ripened loss matched mine.
Two wounds touching start to bleed again.

Wetness is blessed: fountain stubbornly tumbling
to rise again over dust, shit, shards of glass.

"Now I want to kneel at a stream and drink,
or drink from a cup"; words flow from you

the week I'm teaching water, dipping deep
in Walden Pond, cursing aridities.

It had been said before as praise: "Recovered
greenness"; as prayer: "Send my roots rain."

Subterranean fathers hollowly
boom at the bottom of their empty cistern

Drink me. My son's new interest in drains
and water fountains (mountains, as he calls them):

he squats or lies face down to peer below
the grating; stretches up to touch the water.

Mountain of water, shine another spring
so we can drink from you or wet our lips

or raise a chancy cup
and across the rim salute each other's

continued greenness. But the wind blows fresh
and filthy from the river.

Fix what is broken. What is scattered gather.
Easy to say. Not far from here, a woman

looks up to meet her eyes in the mirror
and sees a death. Her own?

Something terrible is about to happen?
Something terrible has already happened.

Not in the dead of winter
her father went, but one day before Easter

he walked the green, the warming earth, then vanished.
Pieces of his shirt still lay on the rug that night

where they'd cut it off to try to start his heart.
The tick, the march, inexorable. She touches

her own heart. It's beating.
Wait. There are children sleeping.

There is unfinished music on the table.
The rest of a life waits on the other side of the mirror

and also somewhere invisible a limit.
A wall. If it were only painted black,

if she could see dark glass, it would be clearer.
She would be able to turn away from light

awhile and walk to the room of the dead and say
it again: Something terrible has happened.

Fix what is broken. What is scattered gather.
Love's gift of agates sown on the barren winter:

find them, restring them in another order.
And news of the lost father—

bottle bobbing, contents still unread,
toward a nameless destination,

perhaps a country where there are no fathers,
far out across the black and oily water.

Swoop of a bird swung between high walls.
Cry of a child rising from the house of darkness.

vii
Up, uppie, says the boy, and holds his arms
up to be lifted in a world where sink
and table, chair and crib are still so tall
they have to be looked up to. Uppie, up!

The small bones lengthen, stretching in his sleep.
He is growing up. Our idiom features
cosily preposition-ended phrases
as well for aging, as *slow down, dry out*,

finally *shrivel up*.
Withered, a bush blows hard in autumn wind,
bald of petals now but still upright,
up, up,
obeying the commands of appetite.

Hortus Conclusus (Spring)

Our walk that Sunday in the mind's kind eye
has mellowed to unmitigated good
(not that from the start there wasn't joy)
like so many days of parenthood.
Days? Hours. Hour. Each bestrollered son
(Jonathan at two and Sam at one)
inaugurates the day by eating jam
cookies at the Hungarian patisserie
across from the Cathedral, while you
and I share cappuccino to go

which I can savor two months later—now.
Can see the leashed white rabbit on the lawn
nibbling while petted, just a step or two
from the huge, ecumenical, brand new
Cathedral fountain's statue. Step back! We
better decode this iconography.
Two praying hands, two Pegasuslike wings;
crab claws; twined flowers; a great smiling face
of sun or moon, if the moon has rays;
and at the top, scaling a horn of plenty,
androgynous Andromeda or saint,
a rescued maiden reaches for the sky.
However overloadedly baroque,
somehow the sense is of serenity,
as what is not, seen from not too close up?

Let's move on. The boys already have,
lacking, so far, a taste for allegory.
Besides, the unfinished fountain is still dry.
Where have they vanished? We both start to run.
Sam's among bushes, chasing a red hen.
Jonathan, standing in a patch of sun,
intercepts crusts of bread a shirtless man
(monk, beggar, saint?) smilingly scatters to
the birds, the boys—all's one. A flash of blue
illuminates the underbrush. Boys, look—
it isn't every day you see a peacock!

See how it struts and preens and juts its head!
All right, don't look. You're hungry; have some bread.
Remember jam from half an hour ago
still smearing your four ruddy cheeks? No? No.

Further from the fountain, a green wall
hides a secret: the enclosed and small
garden whose every plant is biblical.
Luckily this scrawny quince tree shows
no fruit, as yet, to pluck. Two ladies knit
on a stone bench—the same bench where I sat
in early June not quite three years ago
wondering whether the blood test would show
what I already knew or thought I knew—

a memory I might have time to blurt
to you, but Sam starts howling. Is he hurt?
("Sam's crying," Jonathan puts in his two
cents' worth of sober realism to you.)
No, only tired. Heavy-eyed, napward bound,
breaded and jammed, both settle back without a sound,
each in his deckchair taking in the scene,
two tiny passengers finally headed home.

Over the strollers you and I begin
to gather the loose edges up again
of the diffuse long dialogue that we
seem to sustain, however interruptedly,
the gaps and eddies of poetic logic
garbled by two, three, four, six lives' pace
but leapfrogged over by our friendship's magic.
Admittedly most of our talk these days
sounds simply like complaint. I kvetch to you
about the things you kvetch about to me.
With unrehearsed simultaneity
we talk about the damages of time,
how spring feels done and summer coming on.

Trudging home, we trample over rhyme,
vision, perfection, what's impossible
or wishable to try for. Resonance
of acts or names—as parent, poet, teacher—
we both have blindly struggled to attain.

We talk about the blossoming of speech,
substantives learned, subjunctive within reach,
and future beckoning. We even toss
out into sunlight a black label: loss.
Not daily chaos, insufficient sleep:
these are forgotten and recur, to be
again forgotten, though they do chip deep
gradually, invisibly.
I meant more. I meant that when we grow
up into the world is when we start
to wish—no, not to wish—well, to let go.
Each child does its little flaxen bit
to pry us loose, and we begin to die.

The sun's now at the zenith in the sky
above us. In this dance there is no way
to clasp hands with the dead and living equally.
The quick, the dead change places as they can
(do your two half-dead fathers make up one live man?).
Beyond the consolation of our back
and forth, we cast a glance
over our shoulders at the dream
creature rising from the raw
fountain of hope, its waters not yet flowing.
We remember the improbable peacock,
the rabbit unconcernedly
nibbling outside the secret garden. Look:
a new moon bobbing on its length of string
over the broken world.

Suddenly I remember
however deciduous the two
of us may feel, it's spring.
This morning's jaunt—not even half a day,
measured in clock time—was our fumbling way
to celebrate a season which may well
never feel new to us again—no matter.
The boys (both now asleep) deserved an hour,
a day, an instant—oh, the hell with time—
a memory of rabbit, peacock, sun,
statue, jam, or rooster—all by now
receding in a sentimental glow
to the rosy, the unblemished good
one sees (it's pure illusion, God knows how)
when looking back at days of parenthood.

I tell you what I saw. I see it still.
　　Here on this hill
what grows beneath the fingers becomes real.
　　Adjacent towers.
Terrace and garden overlook a waste
　　of ocean, and the wall
that separates the realms is Janus-faced.

One blue-black bronze and one deciduous tree.
　　An inner eye
fixes our houses high above the sea.
　　This was another life:
two worlds, neighboring yet separate.
　　My garden and your courtyard are the key.
To get the vision clear I have to set

a statue in my tower's garden. Stone
　　warmed by each summer's sun,
sturdy, chipped, dependable, benign,
　　silent as a tree,
it seems to have been always standing there
　　through snow and rain.
One day it will disappear.

Your terrace has an empty pedestal
　　that casts a shadow on your polished wall.
Vacancy here is all but visible.
　　Shading your eyes, you peer
down at a tiny ship whose blackened sail
　　punches a hole
in sunlight, as the father cries *I fall*.

Of was it *fail*? *I fail and you fail too*?
　　Don't know. Too few
echoes linger. Children must construe
　　whatever tiny cry,
whatever silence stretches through the years.
　　So I, so you
sit listening in our adjacent towers

for hints and scraps of absences. A frieze
　　to varying degrees
invisible enwraps us in the ways
　　we make, we live.
Now dark wings spread themselves above the work.
　　Now infant eyes
dazzled by daylight miss a ghostly mark.

Speaking of infancy, a pair of children—
　　male, golden—
walk lightly across either place's lawn,
　　past statue, pedestal,
don't notice that the homing sail is black.
　　They recognize the sun.
They are the sun. Moon, take off your cloak!

To be a mother is to be a house
　　he first must trace
a path away from, wander, and embrace
　　her rediscovered shape near story's end.
Circling that statue, I retread the dance.
　　Who's rootless, motherless
can pull away without a backward glance.

Your voice—I heard it on the radio—
　　started as stream and grew
deeper as you approached the center. No
　　center—*ruins*.
Your altar was a husk, a stony core,
　　temple of few
austere gods, and an unfinished stair.

That courage of no center. . . . I gaze down
　　from this walled garden,
try to imagine it in some new form.
　　Do I dare turn my back
on a beloved refuge no new scene
　　could ever with fresh eloquence affirm
and jump into the unknown deep and drown?

Not for me the salt of selflessness.
      I never had a choice.
My suicidal springs are done in place.
      Antaeus touched the earth
and always found his needed strength again.
      It's time to praise
the gentleness of repetition

that takes a longer way around to death.
      Underneath
statue and pedestal an earthy breath
      blows on the bones.
At the cliff's base the sea is blank with noon.
      That urgent wraith
is surfacing: *Come down!*

Better my blackness than a day's white page,
      the piddling wage
life pays to keep you trundling in your cage.
      Eat, sleep, work,
write—that incessant squirming of the palm . . .
      Come down! Assuage
dailiness in my unending calm.

So easy to put words to the dark call.
      Was it a dream, a gull,
a tree's long sighing at the start of fall?
      It comes from my throat too.
Rooted though I am in solid ground,
      tending a horizontal
garden bed, I listen to the sound.

But its solution is too steep for me,
      absolute in its verticality.
Minutes, hours march across the day.
      Our dawn is noon.
Stand on the wall and watch the passing fleet:
      sails ebony against the evening sky
will glow like pearl by morning. Only wait.

See the survivors feasting on the lawn.
  The death's head's gone
back to the cellarage, where ghosts belong.
  We go there too
all in good time. Now celebrate the sun
  sinking as the party lurches on.
The children know it never will be done.

II

Like a huge tree house out of mortal reach,
high platforms thickest foliage nearly hides.
Instead of speech,
hands reach across and down to help us up.
Translation: crossing over an abyss,
handing the little ones, the old ones over
to who'll receive them. Carryings
from here to the ineffable and endless.
Tradition: handing on and handing down
and handing up, a laying on of hands.
Hand over hand pass on, press in
the secret of ascent:
gravity's up. The jungle is too lush
to walk in, so we all find other ways
of navigating: flail, wade, bracchiate,
hooting like happy apes,
or silently, staggeringly, smoothly
swim, angels, fishes, forward through the green
gloom towards a height, a waterfall
or treefall one can climb? A gap; a dome;
more reaching hands; and a pervasive light.

I grope to find the phrases for two thoughts.
One, everything is new—
butterfly   doorknob   toothbrush
         clap your hands
look at the light   the light—

and two, I'm starting to run out of words
for private use. You'd think
that one could give and keep at the same time,
         take through giving,
twin gestures, teaching/mothering: two tasks

you give your blood and brains to and they thank you
by passing plates for more. Okay, okay,
I didn't do it to be thanked. And yet
         the bottom of the barrel
feels perilously close to glinting up.

Crusty tongue. Cups that once held milk.
A mouth begins as organ of ingestion,
then gets its teeth in talk and never stops.
         Cup breast tongue
all provided courtesy of mother.

I never thought of thanking mine for years.
She never made those velvet vocables,
smooth secret treasures, taffy to the palate,
         mine to keep,
in fact my own invention, I knew,

not some old heirloom. Later I let go.
They fell from my open mouth and I live on
to tell the tale again.
         Pass it on.
Keep words and eat them. Don't your eyes light up

equally at *cookie* or any other noun
you recognize?—all goodies you'll hand down,
as the phrase goes, we hope, to your own children.
	A body passes
through a body, changing it forever.

Carry on the torch was what they told me
in high school, i.e. teach; be like your father.
Knowledge, it seemed, was like a relay race.
	I didn't know
the torch would have to pass through my own body.

The gates of truth are ivory and horn,
easily read as irony and horn.
Which is the one for you?
First put your blinders on.
Nothing is surely true,
neither pain nor song.
I wept in Florida a life ago,
saying *I want to always be with you*
and recognizing falsehood even then.
As a criterion no tear will do
as true heart's key, as visionary gleam;
no brimming eyes, no wet dream;
no thrill as hairs along the forearms rise.
What quickens pulse, shakes knees
is the sheer staggering blindness of the choice,
secret—the wellsprings of an inner voice
that rises to the threshold of the throat
struggling to utter its one note.

Teaching Emily Dickinson

What starts as one more Monday morning class
merges to a collective Dickinson,
separate vessels pooling some huge truth
sampled bit by bit by each of us.

She sings the pain of loneliness for one.
Another sees a life of wasted youth;
then one long flinching from what lay beneath
green earth; last, pallid peerings at the stone

she too now knows the secret of.

                                        Alone,
together, we'd decipher BIRD   SOUL   BEE
dialect humdrum only until heard
with the rapt nervy patience, Emily,
you showed us that we owed you. One small bird
opens its wings. They spread. They cover us:
myriad lives foreshortened into Word.

The filling that yesterday worked itself loose from your tooth
sits on the shelf, the sink, the bedside table

like Amfortas' portable wound in Syberberg's *Parsifal*,
a plug compounded of craft and pain,

compact enough to clasp in a palm.
Today our capital city's endless bland

facades as we pace mile on marble mile
strike me as divorced from any meaning

except their own monumentality.
Nor is it just immensity. Mycenae

worn shiny as fangs with use
is pillaged of context, shrunken to silence.

Nothing left to see but skeleton.
Nothing will leap the boundaries of bone.

I clasp your hand. We push through cold spring wind
down the flowering avenue of deaths.

What are these signs embellishing the new
black cenotaph we come on last? Its dark

plainness has left nothing to be robbed
and everything—the freight of names—to time.

i

Symbols, messages the aging hand
scribbles at midnight and no one will read.
The story of Frau Haydn
using her husband's music scores
to line her pastry pans
must be apocryphal, it turns up so often
(Massinger's plays); yet no less true for that?
Hours fill up with absent-minded humming.
Drafts cross the floor; a cat's paw
slips under the door unseen.
Everywhere the inner skeleton edges
closer to the surface.

ii

Unmake, remake the self? This means assuming
not that the center holds
but that there is a center.
Ideas of the eternal harden, cool;
lava petrifies to posture. Me
myself I only know what brims, what spills,
stretches, or shrinks, by pain—
not pain exactly; knowing something's wrong.
Triumphantly the dowser,
however deep the treasure lies, cries *Water!*
touching the magical, the buried fault:
a moment ritual cannot suffice.

iii

A world to which return is not so much
impossible as futile: Iason, slate-eyed,
wounded in the Korean War, drove taxis;
his wife was crippled by a fall; his daughter
Katerina always dressed in black,
mourning for whom I never learned. All this
I see too clearly still to wish for further
intercourse with who I thought they were,

who (a greater riddle) they thought I was.
Who *I* thought I was I no longer care. . . .
Returning bottles to the Lesbian deli,
I'm asked if I will teach the baby Greek.

iv

Eve caused the whole fucking problem
says a man in a group in the park
as I trudge by pushing the stroller.
He capers, nearly dances with conviction.
Women and children cause the world to fall.
These mothers bending at the sandbox bars
wear their weariness into the future,
feed their children *mine* and *more* with milk—
the coming generation, the old story
Eve started. In my yellow dress, I pick
a dandelion, hand it to the baby
whose fallen nature blights the soft new grass.

v

We had no time to lay the cornerstone before
the place was dynamited
down to its foundations. All the data
needed to build with symmetry, proportion
floated away, time capsule
light and insouciant as a balloon.
The building on the ruined site
was to have been named for you,
but I forget your name. You pointed up
at all the vanishing artifacts
free as a balloon whose string is cut
and you said: Moon.

Lilacs look neon in fading light.
Death makes life shine:
a tiredness, a flickering between

ages, which is each age;
a piling up to tottering
and falling back to sand.

So much for cycle. The front door lock
sticks each fall when we're first back.
We are advised to oil it.

Olive oil in the keyhole:
again the old key turns.
Once again to meander

along the edge of water,
whether tideless sea or tidal river,
pushing the stroller, dreaming

oil in the lock; the key
dipped in lubricity
the boychild's shining skin
me tired to the bone

Already summer's over.
Goodbye, lilacs. Your
neon is past; you'll bloom again

next spring. Past an age
each season feels like an end of summer
but still the tale's to tell

over and over for those
lolling and snoozing in the stroller,
preparing to come after.

Tall house standing on its high green hill—
children, do you remember?
Lawns slant down to a stream.

Under a striped tent
a buffet's spread in the sun.
Ideas of the eternal,

once molten, harden; cool.
Oil, oil in the lock.
The old key turns.

Teaching the text, I feel
the little hairs along my forearms rise
and shield my eyes
against the nimble letters on the page.
They spell a man
who weeps and weeps alone
for his brief golden age.
Presently the line where sea meets sky
fills with silhouetted men. An army
deployed behind him comes between
margin and horizon like a screen
on which hexameters drum down like rain.

Velocity, one of my students calls you—
notably a quality you lacked.
Your virtues were in rootedness. Another
student says loser (losers get marooned);
another scumbag, with that puss-drenched foot.
Your filthy wound offends their pristine senses?

It took a god swung in on a high crane,
awkwardly booming, to proclaim you free
to turn tail and escort the mumbling boy
back, first across a too familiar sea,
then to the old scene, Troy.
No other power could deflect that pull

of cord strung taut, Odysseus to the child,
tangled in you, your festering foot, your root
and rooted tentacle of sour attachment.
The cliff, cave, trees; the stream; your slice of sky
loved through the ten ineffable (how not?)
years: it was to these you said goodbye

when after so much silence you heard language,
heard Greek again, but put to what vile use.
Worse than the bow: that they could snatch from you
and turn against you, but the subtle tongues,
so many serpents coiling in their nests,
spitefully hissing plots to bring Troy down,

to bring you back! No; turn your back on them,
address the hills, the ether, all that's pure
and utterly ungiving as untaking.
Sun circled sky, moon rose, week followed week,
yet dreams (home; vengeance) visited in Greek.
Ten years you held to emptiness. No more.

The boy on the neighboring table asks to hold
his fresh-filled blood-bag up.
He presses it to his cheek.
Mine, mine, all out of me, he says. *Still warm!*
Kiss it goodbye, I comment inwardly.

Pass it on. Nothing is yours to keep.
Cold February outside; hot heart's blood
inside, a sum of absence drained, bagged,
ready to be piped on.
The dark sack bulges. Dirty work of habit done

or doing, as I learn to sleep alone.
The eyes, those windows of the soul,
still brim with dreams,
absently contemplate the snow
they open to. Lips too

swollen with unspoken
syllables lie, blood-warm,
one on one, unopening
until there's more to say
than snow-blurred dawn already turning brown.

Cold nights when I began
to imagine the blazing world as a layer of frost
I wouldn't willingly crack.
Lips to the warm, the inmost icicle,
I curled back up, dreaming of young men

huddled around a fire to keep warm.
White ash kiss awakening to snow
some sleeping beauty? No—
seal of a crystal, shattered, mended, whole.
Then sleep again, dark freighter on the sluggish blood canal.

Dream-gifts' insistent signal: beauty, youth,
dangerous mountain country to be crossed
at altitudes of sheer exhilaration,
the precipice you never thought to touch
suddenly within reach.

So touch. And the response—
barriers broken, borders
breached in the sleeper's brimming nonchalance—
awakens white
unveilings of the curtains of the night.

Those early morning classes—it was rough.
I'd clear my throat. I didn't want to sing;
simple gabble would have been enough.
And yet the miracle kept happening,
September to October to November,
morning by morning, up to mid-December.

I guess I improvised. I learned to swing
over the thickets of the syllabus,
acres of scrub assigned to me to cover,
with a grand gesture. Apelike, I would gibber.
I'd pluck the choicest fruits and gently stuff
those doubtful mouths with goodies. From the dim

lecture-hall/jungle they would gape at me—
annoyed, alert, aghast, how could I see?
I didn't want to know. I wanted them
to stay awake, though. One good stratagem
was to alarm them into some new way
of thought. Conspiratorially I'd say:

"You think I'm here to bore you—as I may.
But children, children, it is not just I
who am balanced here precariously.
We're all suspended between life and death—
I perching here and you who crowd beneath.
We're teetering, every one, at an abyss.

If from my fragile perch I seem ridiculous,
remember that my task's to give a clue,
some clue you can remember, to a past
you never knew, spectacular and vast,
and also to a future that I pray
we'll live to taste. Life's not one dull day."

I could embroider on the fantasy,
but clock and calendar cruelly, mercifully
tell me to stop. I stop. A scrape of chairs.
Subdued or sleepy, they all trail downstairs.
That seeming raptness may well be all lies,
but how I miss the glint of many eyes!

The term is done then. Silence smothers me
surprisingly. I'd thought that I would be
grateful to rest, shut up, take a vacation.
But not teaching is terrible. I sing
softly to myself and wait for spring.
This megalomania must be my vocation.

Generations

i

How well I understand it now, my father's
dumbshow pointing, tragicomic reaching
for salt or butter. Too much trouble to
find the words for whatsitsname when your
anonymous familiars know your needs.
No need of endless labels. Today the baby
points to my shoe, says *Mama's*—
articulating that apostrophe.
He calls for ham and raisins, not because
he wants them, though he does. Rather it's that
the words wait, shining virgins, for his use.

ii

Bathroom scale, thermometer are *ock*
for clock. And *ock* is also hot; block; box; socks.
Nin means pin, *ninny* for short, and *nen*
means pen or pencil. *Gok*: dog. *Guk*: milk.
Mama and Daddy are self-evident
and Grandma has no name and then is Amma.
Aisin: raisin. *Asses*: glasses. *Io*: cheerio.
Bubble is bubble, whether blown in play,
or drops of water in the bath, or bits
of dandelion fluff that, puffed at, float away.

iii

So as he picks up language's long-shadowing
spear and brandishes it recklessly,
I'm sinking mildly into the resigned
dumbness of middle age. Had known some such
chiasmus would be coming, but so fast!
Pale and solemn, shadowed by the tent's
lurid red and yellow stripes, he rides
the carousel at the Kiwanis Carnival
around and around. Perched on the neighboring horse
sidesaddle, I just manage not to touch
his hands that tightly clutch the pole. His head.

iv

Some experts find the fear of nuclear
annihilation foremost in the minds
of children; other claim that we project
our terrors onto their unconsciousness,
the true concerns of kids being narcissistic.
Why shouldn't both be right? We live in heaven,
spy hell in lurid cracks. We live in hell,
preferring not to dwell too morbidly
on our condition. Double-natured, we
thirst for the ease of dream and fable, food
and mirror, money, ivory, and horn.

v

Focussing on zero, you look
at it and at it and finally through it
and see a tiny chiselled nameless thing
lying at the bottom of a well
or anywhere sky and water meet.
Then sky turns dark and smoky.
A thin black line stretches from end to end
for us to dance across
from pole to pole, believing, not believing,
having no choice but to entrust ourselves
to the torqued embrace of twin impossibles.

vi

After the Chinese food and beer and kisses of reunion,
sleepily we talk of death and birth,
of terror and of comfort, their equation:
grandmother dying of cancer,
baby astir in the womb.
A cockroach crawls in the beer mug.
The cat with the ulcered ear
purring reaches up a paw to knead
the beard of the father-to-be
who soon will dive from his fragile tower
into an unfathomed blood-warm sea.

vii

We sit and cogitate our common lot,
each of us remembering, foreseeing
those deaths we know the best. Outlined, macabre,
the child in the sonogram seems to shake her fist.
And in the chic boutique you've told me of,
a teddy bear winds up to white womb noises—
amnio growls to soothe the savage breast
of a new creature thrust bald and wild
into such a weirdly silent world?
Latest in lullabies, bubble and squeak
of guts, lub-dub of the maternal heart.

viii

Scattered in play over the lawn, these beans
(*neens*, says the baby) oddly root and tangle
in the matted turf. Not odd—stubborn.
They want to live. And lovely fragile poppies,
great petals tousled by one day of rain,
droop in the shaggy border.
But I was thinking of the beans—
inscrutable containers, possibilities
by the handful (one was black, one white),
popping in grass and in my head at night,
crammed with meaning, coded for the future.

ix

Toddler in nursing home, cooings predicted—
so weak the link between imagination and event.
Two caged lovebirds chitter and flirt in the lobby
(bronze; marble; mirrors; the only mirrors here).
Upstairs he does look; smile; say "Amma"; then
dashes immediately from the room
into the hall. Explore! Patrol! Discover
for whom that goll keeps tolling (goll = bell).
They may have shared some signs of recognition
unequally. She can't reach out to him;
sheer quicksilver, he cannot sit still.

X

Flies in amber? Something viscous, heavy,
transparent, gradually hardens
around them, slows them down
at last to utter immobility.
Those who still live must struggle to wade through it,
totter (Time's stilts, said Proust). No energy
to spare for signs of recognition. Only
a few, incarcerated by mistake,
claw at the translucent envelope.
You and I, younger, move more freely through
our thickening matrix. Naked, the baby flies.

III

Summer in White, Green, and Black

In the beginning summer stretches out
like one enormous sheet
of whitest paper, but ideas of white
grow overlaid with leaves,
become an avenue that desires shade,
ramify, trembling. . . . Leaf-shaped shadows waver.
Enchanted, slow,
the stroller glides along this avenue
where waving branches cancel out the high
hot glare of summer sky.
Soon long exposure to
such generosity of green
turns the white page a sickly eye-ease shade,
then pale bland black
like asphalt freshly spread:
smooth, soft, all but sticky in the heat,
seeming pristine but not
new, just a latest coat.

The leaves are shaking as before a storm.
All of them will fall, but later on.
Earliest shudderings stipple the white
page already piecemeal into air—
absorbed, clean gone.
Summer is done. The white
page might almost never have been there
but for this surface offered you to write.

Back in the country, too
   happy to fall asleep
this first night. Buried summers
   keep me up

like a hillside of stone
   where one long quartzite tooth
points from grassy green
   its gleaming truth.

An all-embracing web
   threaded from room to room,
memory looping myth,
   touches not me alone

but all who breathe here, sigh,
   creak, remember, dream.
Is that a monstrous bat
   bumping against the screen?

If I commit myself
   to turning out the light,
the panicky bump-bump
   will relocate

inside my skull. Too
   happy here to fall
asleep, my jackknifed friend,
   or not at all

happy? These words are two
   sides of a single coin
flipping itself for hours
   in my old room.

Simply being alive
   is keeping me awake.
If sleep's a little death,
   why dive into the dark?

Opposites baffle me.
    The country's what is real.
Here's where I drive a car,
    put hands in soil;

and nothing here seems real.
    It all accumulates
grotesquely: mason jars,
    memories, straw hats,

tins of dried-up tea,
    shells from some dry sea . . .
just to unpack means raising thick
    clouds of *nostalgie*.

Everything's gone beyond
    limits. The trees have grown
far past the planter's purpose. Deep
    shadows stripe the lawn.

Finally everything
    will fall apart, corrupt,
dear bodies sifting back to soil;
    but that keeps me awake

too! As we age and age,
    I like to catch us at it.
May no natural change for me
    ever seem automatic.

The blossoming of trees,
    lilacs late into May—
it takes me hours of moonlight
    to understand one day,

the first day of our summer.
    Our son's first summer here
shoots him up to boldness
    and down to sheer

frustration. Doorknobs; stairs;
    grass higher than his head;
great ants; a rake; a trowel;
    bare feet on a dirt road;

flowers to warm his hands at;
    lunches of bread and jam;
he doesn't say *I'm happy*.
    He lives *I am*

all day. All day, all night
    in my childhood's room
we wear our bodies deeper
    and deeper into time.

Bats, it appears, have had an awful press.
More people get killed at church
picnics each year by lightning
than annually die of bat-borne rabies,
says the column B clipped and sent,
instructing me in things I'd long ignored
or tried to disregard:
bad bat statistics mix
with the taste of last night's choucroute,
the Duchess apples daily ripening, you
naked and golden, rolling
over the tattered crazy-quilt
that smells of ancient cat-pee.
And now I've candied you in poetry.

False. No summer afternoon's its own
radiant, miniature story.
All the lawns of August fail to show
a monumental cliff, its bas-relief
waist deep in water and so far illegible;
to show how you in your blue pointed hood
fell swiftly down a well,
down, down beneath the surface of the earth
and vanished; to show me
watching as you fell;
and how proleptic absence struck
its long reverberation, a black bell.

Anything could be lost. Could be and will be.
See, here I bring you back.
I hold you now this gray March afternoon
tightly against my neck.
Last summer's apples ripened, fell. The quilt
comes apart bit by bit. Choucroute
was savored and digested and is gone.
Bats bite their rare victims
and lightning strikes at the picnic
always somewhere else
only so long; then rattles

its way to the startled heart.
Memory will be powerless to retrieve
what's lost, yet this crazy
poise is what we have:
teetering on the edge,
thrusting our heads into,
out of the empty tank,
insisting on the truth of what is gone.

The Writing on the Wall

Pools of dryness spread behind the eyes
of signs and eyes that scan the season's windows.
Use water wisely warns
the sign above the faucet.
And on milk cartons, subways, station walls:

Have you seen these missing children?
Faces, braces, names,
birthdates, last dates seen
pull people toward
data they gaze at, pull away again.

Surface tensions daily
toughen, scrape, and thin the public skin.
Open shut eyes take in
the riddle that the moon—
silent, defiant, sleepless—

is posting past the corner of the night.
Drought threatens. Oh clear sky,
all things go near the bone.
In a warm whirlpool I
kissed my friend to welcome his new son.

A wise use? Or a waste,
to greet and hold what other people lose?
For eyes that see,
the moon's white bowl of possibility
shines into the unprotected house.

The Burial of Jonathan Brown
1983–1985

So many memories: sun, snow, and rain,
the age-old alteration, white to green.
You do not tire of living;
things go new again.
Takers turn late to giving.

This boy's blond flame
wavers in buggy grass
or lights his shadowed room.
The baffled dog sniffs, remembers him.
What is gone,

cheating departure, stays
imprinted on your days.
You thought of him as summer growing tall.
Foreknowledge of a life
would be a dreadful gift.

April, May: earth loosens up her lap
again. The thaw
receives this flesh
eight seasons saw.
You plant his name

trustingly in time;
cry for more, more
to fill the flawed
frame of hours,
arms clasping empty years,

and there is no more
beyond human love.
He came from that;
now he returns to what
becomes of winter in the warm new air.

Giving him up,
filling in the spot,
you put him back.
The hill goes green
with his name.

i

Of all the times when not to speak is best,
mother's and infant's is the easiest,
the milky mouth still warm against her breast.

Before a single year has passed, he's well
along the way: language has cast its spell.
Each thing he sees now has a tale to tell.

A wide expanse of water = ocean. Look!
Next time, it seems that water is a brook.
The world's loose leaves, bound up into a book.

ii

The habit holds for love. He wants to seize
lungsful of ardent new sublimities.
Years gradually pry him loose from these.

He comes to prize a glance's eloquence,
learning to construct a whole romance
from hint and gesture, meaning carved from chance.

And finally silence. Nothing in a phrase
so speaks of love as an averted gaze,
sonnets succumbing to remembrances.

iii

At the Kiwanis travelling carnival
I ride beside you on the carousel.
You hold on solemnly, a little pale.

I don't stretch out my hand. You ride alone.
Each mother's glance reduplicates my own:
the baffled arc, the vulnerable bone.

Myself revolving in the mirror's eye
as we go round beneath a cloudy sky,
eyeing my little boy attentively,

I swallow what I was about to say
(no loving admonition is the way
to bridge this gap) and hear the music play

and later, wordless, reach and lift you down
over the rigid horse's shiny brown
mane, and press your body close against my own.

Stillness after motion,
the creaky music cranking, cranking down,
the carnival preparing to leave town.

You lean across the table
and ask me about anger.

Immediately I picture
a ball of crud dung beetles
industriously roll
across the inner eye's proscenium.
The cake of dung is solid and cohesive,
its separate ingredients
hard to disengage,
strands of being human knotted solid.

I'm nothing but an amateur at anger.
I recognize its symptoms
and often cannot summon
courage to call by name
this presence, this glum guest,
this energy, this pain,
this first word of the Iliad, this friend.

Festering millennia
have passed and here we are:
anger locked in the chest
exactly where Homer left it.
Inside the shaggy breast
how the hot heart divides
into one part of rage
and one part that makes song.

Impatience taps a foot.
Contempt stifles a sigh.
The soul is left alone
to meet an outer eye,

eye of a daisy tossed
(*loves me/loves me not*)
onto the ground, its auguries
trampled underfoot.
The final petal still
intact, the tale untold,
we cry for happy endings
until our lips grow cold.

i

A summer spent rehearsing,
we've still not found the way.
We tried idolatry,
fighting the tendency of everything
not invisible to disappear.
Jonathan started, calling the wind blue.
I take it up: summer began as red
and cooked to a curdled spectrum
of dried blood (bug bite, paper cut)
to brown (old brick) and finally
barn boards blushing gray.
What we can name is ours to keep. We dodge
the translucent label marked Goodbye.

ii

Looking at his version of Noah's Ark,
"I don't like the dove leaving," says J.
"It found a home," I say.
"Picture it nesting in an olive tree."
"But it's not *in* the picture."

                              I agree.
Happy endings fudge our deepest fears,
beg questions, break the laws
of leavetaking. We *know* the dove was lost
over the waste of waters.

Goldilocks clattered panicky downstairs
and raced into the forest, so the bears
(who wanted to be friendly, we are told)
had no chance to wave their puzzled paws.

iii

Courage to speak? be still?
to go away? to stay?
Courage to listen to the colorless.
There is no way of giving the wind color
yet everything has voice and speaks as wind
when wind speaks. And we listen.
Courage of listening. Of admitting loss.
The small dark cat, dead, buried
brown in the pinewoods, dumb
earth tamped flat with a thump—
no requiescat. Nothing left to say.
And woke to find a single word
drying its wings on my lips.

iv

Hello is almost as difficult as Goodbye
and more embarrassing, although less tragic.
Deprived of both these greetings,
Orpheus understandably confused them,
unable to believe a horrid blank
could serve as passage to a new beginning.
I get it wrong at the start.
My friend is coming towards me.
We recognize each other
and lift our hands and wave
to bridge the middle distance.
Always I wound her by my lack of warmth,
my insufficient eagerness to leap over
the remaining space between us.

V

It takes this room without a window for
the light of Ormos mornings to shine back
unquenchable. It takes this mirrorless
mustard-walled waiting room to set in place
the frame of lamplit bodies' long embrace.
It takes the clock one has to crane to see
to measure private hours for you and me—
hours in abeyance, past or yet to come.
Away from home we long for home.

Language condenses into poetry,
essentially a cry
also sometimes called apostrophe
that boils down to two syllables, goodbye—
a word there's no right way to say.

Sweet smell of phlox drifting across the lawn—
an early warning of the end of summer.
August is fading fast, and by September
the little purple flowers will all be gone.

Season, project, and vacation done.
One more year in everybody's life.
Add a notch to the old hunting knife
Time keeps testing with a horny thumb.

Over all these months hung an unspoken
aura of urgency. In late July
galactic pulsings filled the midnight sky
like silent screaming, so that, strangely woken,

we looked at one another in the dark,
then at the milky magical debris
arcing across, dwarfing our meek mortality.
There were two ways to live: get on with work,

redeem the time, ignore the imminence
of cataclysm; or else take it slow,
be as tranquil as the neighbors' cow
we love to tickle through the barbed-wire fence
(she paces through her days in massive innocence,
or, seeing green pastures, we imagine so).

In fact, not being cows, we have no choice.
Summer or winter, country, city, we
are prisoners from the start and automatically,
hedged in, harangued by the one clamorous voice.

Not light but language shocks us out of sleep—
ideas of doom transformed to meteors
we translate back to portents of the wars
looming above the nervous watch we keep.

Love—its long spoon, its promise, and its threat—
you won't go empty, I shall make you eat,
        I'll fend off death—
apostrophizes an averted face,
retreats with a reluctant backward glance.

Agitated wings
flap at the cold containment of the moon,
        fluttering
batlike, bewildered out of a dark cave
and bump themselves on light's solidity

as on an arm outstretched in utter trust,
patient as trees, pouring itself, until
        ethereal
it has been drained of every precious cell
to share with who may happen to be dry.

A house of appetite and sustenance
links, shelters, and divides
        inhabitants who feed,
work, walk together and as in a dream
undoing the loose bonds of need float free.

You and I, walking toward this silent house,
encounter no warm gold
        ring of lantern light
such as draws chilly travellers and moths.
No lamp burns here but blood,

mortal fuel consumed at steady speed.
Ghosts in disappointment flit away,
        hunger unsatisfied.
Dim in the room we turn to one another,
open our lips, and speak

a single word and raise a mutual finger.
Into such stillness no new thing should spill,
            muddy the mirror
we turn our double back to speechlessly
and sit and eat our fill.